TEACHING IN TOUGH TIMES

TEACHING IN TOUGH TIMES

ENCOURAGEMENT FOR TODAY'S TEACHER

JUDY NICHOLS

Baker Books

A Division of Baker Book House Co
Grand Rapids, Michigan 49516

Published by Baker Books
a division of Baker Book House Company
P.O. Box 6287, Grand Rapids, MI 49516-6287

Printed in the United States of America

Library of Congress Cataloging-in-Publication Data

Nichols, Judy, 1941–
    Teaching in tough times : encouragement for today's teacher / Judy Nichols.
       p. cm.
    ISBN 0-8010-1146-9 (cloth)
    1. Problem children—Education—United States. 2. Nichols, Judy, 1941– 3. Teachers—United States—Biography. 4. Teachers—Religious life—United States. I. Title.
LC4802.N53 1997
371.93—dc21   97-25290

For current information about all releases from Baker Book House, visit our web site:

http://www.bakerbooks.com

For their loving support and encouragement,
I dedicate this book to
my son, Jim, and my siblings, Larry, Susie, and James

CONTENTS

CONTENTS

PREFACE

Teenage boys crawl out the classroom window to buy drugs from the pusher on the corner. An eleven-year-old girl feeds and diapers her baby before she comes to school. A fifteen-year-old boy who can't read a third grade book skips school to make $1000 a day selling drugs.

I didn't read about these students in college textbooks. I met them, and dozens like them, in a state correctional institution, a private school for juvenile offenders, and two inner city public schools.

My career for the past twenty-two years as a librarian and reading specialist has been primarily in urban settings. In these environments violence, crime, and racial tensions magnified the stress and frustrations of teaching.

When I didn't think I could make it one more day, I'd say a prayer and hang on. My prayers were always answered, often in unexpected ways, as my Lord, Jesus Christ, molded me into a more caring teacher. What I learned in academic courses didn't usually work with at-risk kids. Often the reverse strategy was more effective. I developed the courage to do what I felt was right even if it didn't agree with current research. I wanted my students to succeed in school, not on the street.

For both elementary and secondary students, I taught concepts in concrete, visual ways to catch their interest. Their attitudes and performance improved with contests and rewards; simple, hands-on materials; and a grading system that emphasized their strengths.

My students helped me realize the power of being a loving teacher with Jesus as my master. Writing this book has been a healing experience because their wounds have become part of my own history, etched like stone carvings in my memory.

Today similar situations and students like those I encountered are present in all types of schools across America. I pray this book will help teachers working in tough times and in tough places to call on our Lord, Jesus Christ, for strength, courage, and hope.

PART 1

STATE CORRECTIONAL INSTITUTION FOR JUVENILE OFFENDERS

I am not saying this because I am in need, for I have learned to be content whatever the circumstances.

Philippians 4:11

The abrupt change in environment overwhelmed me when I left a suburban elementary school for a job as a librarian in a large state institution for male offenders, ages twelve to twenty-one. Suddenly I was working in a system that required constant monitoring and extreme caution in the use of supplies and keys. Scissors, ballpoint pens, and cleaning solutions were considered potential weapons and had to be locked up when not in use.

I provided school library services and maintained a staff library in criminal justice, psychology, and education. A guard was on duty in the library during school hours to protect me and to prevent fights. As part of a behavioral modification system, all staff members had to write up positive behaviors and attitudes on slips of paper. These were converted to tokens, which could be used for candy bars, sodas, and other rewards.

The young men, convicted of rape, murder, armed robbery, drug possession, and other crimes, came for prison terms varying from three months to several years. They lived in dorms and came to the main building for classes during the day to earn the GED (Graduate Equivalency Diploma), take high school courses, and work on basic skills.

It was difficult to work with young people who were depressed or hostile. As I began to learn about their histories, I saw how child abuse and neglect can affect a person's development. Their childhoods were often devoid of innocence and play, structure, and love.

I grew spiritually in this setting because the status symbols of the secular world were unimportant here. This enabled me to see beyond the facades and know what a person was really like. Behind a student's angry face, I could often see a lonely, hurting person.

Because there was tremendous pressure working in this high-risk setting, I felt as if I was getting out of prison when I left this job. I developed more compassion and understanding for difficult students and became a strong believer in helping children succeed during the preschool and elementary years.

I dream of the day when young people who are involved in criminal activity will be targeted early for rehabilitation and will be able to improve in a positive environment. In a jail or prison, they usually get worse.

MASQUERADE

The LORD seeth not as man seeth: for man looketh on the
outward appearance, but the LORD looketh on the heart.
1 Samuel 16:7 KJV

Lord, when you sent me
to this prison,
I didn't expect
a masquerade.

Rage cloaked
in depression,
kindness wrapped
in a shell,
hurt tattooed
in a scar.

My students' eyes
reflect stormy emotions.
    "Nobody loves me.
    Nobody cares.
    You don't care either.
    You're like all the rest."
They don't know
I have my own prisons.

Lord,
you can change
emptiness to wholeness,
hate to love,
lost souls into
lively spirits.

Remove the
masks
with
your master key.

Miller came to the library every day to read, listen to tapes, and watch films. He was a winner in the library's poetry contest and enjoyed talking about books that he was reading. Sometimes he brought his guitar and sang soft ballads. It was hard to believe that he'd committed crimes, because the person I knew was sensitive and kind.

"Read his file," the psychiatrist told me. "You'll be surprised." The institutional files, which were kept under lock and key, were filled with educational, psychological, and legal information. As I read Miller's file, I was shocked that he'd killed his stepfather with a shotgun and had no apparent remorse. Although his crime was horrible, it was easier to understand after I read that the stepfather had beaten Miller from an early age while his mother watched in silence.

Behind this teenager's gentle demeanor was a tormented, angry side. The prisons of low self-esteem, child abuse, and guilt held a tighter grip on Miller than the confines of the correctional institution. I could only pray that someday he'd find Jesus, who could offer the forgiveness and love to set his spirit free.

SNAPSHOTS

And Jesus saith unto him, I will come and heal him.
Matthew 8:7 KJV

Snapshots
from his life
make a
tattered scrapbook.

His father disappeared
when he was three.
On his fifth birthday,
his mother died
of an overdose.

Foster homes
glue his
elementary years
into captions
of neglect and loneliness.

Basic skills
flick across
his mind like
flashbulbs,
leaving spaces.

Each day
he enters a darkroom
at school,
exposing undeveloped
film.

Anthony was finally locked up after numerous scrapes with the law. He had stolen cars, committed armed robbery, and sold drugs. He liked to talk about how he skipped high school classes to go out on the street.

"I can make $1000 a day slinging drugs," he told me. "I buy groceries, get presents for my little brother and sister, and give money to my mom for clothes. My mom knows what I'm doing. She gives me a kiss before I leave in the morning and says to be careful."

Anthony was fifteen, and he and his former girlfriend already had a two-year-old son. "She moved away and won't let me see him," he said. "That's because I don't give her much money."

He told me that guys selling drugs don't want to work.

"It gets worse on the streets every year," Anthony said. "I know nine- and ten-year-olds who are selling drugs and stealing cars."

"Don't you want your high school diploma?" I asked.

"I don't think about it. I've had a reading problem since first grade, so I always tried to be the class clown. The teachers would tell me to do my work, and I wouldn't pay no attention. I stopped trying because all I ever got was Fs anyway."

I asked Anthony if he believed in God.

He said, "Yeah, but I'll probably go to hell. I know what I'm doing is wrong. I just can't stop."

When I told Anthony that I would pray for him, he looked surprised. After all, he was locked up with guys who boasted about their crimes.

One day I overheard him bragging to another inmate about how much money he can make in a day. Then he looked at me and acted embarrassed that I had heard him.

The next day he said to me, "When I get out, I'm going to go straight. I'm going to get a job and finish school."

I've heard this comment many times from other students, and I know how difficult it is for them to change. Since Anthony won't be able to read the application very well, it's hard to imagine what kind of job he could get, especially one that pays $1000 a day, tax-free.

RUNAWAYS

Come to me, all you who are weary and burdened, and I
will give you rest.

Matthew 11:28

They disappear
like pencil points
in crowded classrooms,
waiting
to cross the margin.

Climbing and running
punctuate
their sentences
when no one
is looking.

One guard
with clipboard
notices empty
spaces and pursues
an explanation.

The alarm sounds.
Police officers
and guards scatter
like dots
on a page.

The final grade:
withdrawn,
erased on the street,
or returned for another
dull assignment.

In the prison, we called our students by their last names. This was an institutional practice, done purposely to dehumanize them and discourage emotional attachments.

But Rivera broke the prison barriers with his appealing, outgoing personality. Although he had a temper, all the teachers felt he was one of the few who could be successfully rehabilitated.

One day word spread rapidly that two boys had escaped. We were surprised to learn that one of them was Rivera. They were typical runaways, making a desperate plea for help to see if we cared enough to want them back.

We never got a chance to show Rivera and the other boy that we cared. In the cold institutional environment, it wasn't an easy task. That night the boys stole a car. In a high-speed chase with police, they hit a tree and were killed instantly.

Tragedies such as this were not uncommon in the institution, but staff members always wondered if there was something we could have said or done to prevent them. Often it seemed as if the causes were beyond our control: abuse, the street culture, and the wrong friends.

Why do some kids make it while others don't? There is no simple answer, but too often we criticize young people who act bizarre, violent, or different instead of trying to understand them. I will always believe that one caring teacher who sees beyond outward appearances and helps unlock potential can change a young person's life.

HE CAN'T REMEMBER

I will instruct you and teach you in the way you should go;
I will counsel you and watch over you.

Psalm 32:8

He can't remember
    his real parents,
    how many homes he's lived in,
    the friends he left behind.

He can't remember
    the schools he attended,
    the names of his teachers,
    the social workers who tried to help.

He can't remember
    his math facts,
    simple weights and measures,
    how to sound out new words.

Give me the patience
    to help him
    learn something
    worth remembering.

22

When we did biography projects in the library, Ramos wrote a life story that broke my heart. He had never seen his dad. During his first ten years, he and his mom had moved from one dumpy apartment to another. She was an alcoholic and had been evicted for not paying the rent.

At the age of ten, Ramos was taken away from his mother and put in a foster home. Several foster homes later, he had become a thief. First, he started stealing food because he was hungry. For the past two years, he'd been stealing cars and robbing stores.

He had repeated several grades in elementary school. When he reached eighth grade, he was three years older than his classmates. Now he was "institutionalized," meaning he was content with the prison routine because there was no one waiting for him on the outside.

When I had a "Design a Bookmark" contest in the library, he won first prize. He drew a humorous sketch of two inmates in black and white prison uniforms sitting in a cell reading a legal dictionary. The slogan said, "Now that you have all the time in the world, read a book!" When I gave Ramos a certificate, two candy bars, and a new magazine as a prize, he grinned and said, "This is the first time I've ever won anything in my life!"

THE GANGBANGER

Jesus answered them, "It is not the healthy who need a doctor, but the sick. I have not come to call the righteous, but sinners to repentance."

Luke 5:31–32

He's a gangbanger,
doing time for his gang,
a way of walkin'
 and talkin',
 and signifying
that shows
 he's proud
 of where
he came from
and what he's accomplished.

"I just felt
like killin' somebody
that day. Why have a weapon
if I'm not going to use it?
Besides,
I have a reputation
to live up to."

This student
frightens me.
Nothing I say or do
seems to
have an impact.

Somewhere
deep inside him,
you see possibilities
for a new life,
a spirit ripe for healing.

Work
a miracle, Lord.
Your touch is
beyond
my human
understanding.

Jennings is typical of a gang member "doin' time for his gang." It's like a badge of honor because his identity and values are wrapped up with his gang, not his real family. He is out of touch with his feelings, hardened by the street, and unable to empathize with others.

I'm always trying to fix students like Jennings with my handy bag of teacher tricks. I recommend a book that I think will help. I praise, encourage, and lecture. I imagine that if I say or do the right thing, a student who makes me feel uncomfortable will suddenly improve. But troubled kids' problems aren't as simple as I want to make them.

I need to feel their pain along with them and not be so quick to criticize or react to their strange behavior or comments. I believe that Jesus suffers along with us, so why is it such a struggle for me to follow his example?

Listening and understanding without making judgments is difficult for a teacher, especially when a certain student seems possessed by the devil. I need to put away my bag of tricks and love and accept these kids, no matter what their faults. It's amazing how much they calm down and listen when I do.

LOCKED UP

The LORD is good, a refuge in times of trouble. He cares for those who trust in him.

Nahum 1:7

"I'm locked in here
on holidays and weekends,
pretending to be upset
when I hear
about furloughs,
girlfriends,
and going home.

Deep inside
I'm glad
I can't leave.
My mom's a drunk,
my dad doesn't care,
my old friends
have moved away.

Guess I'll celebrate
with an
institutional meal,

27

an old movie,
and a trip to the chapel.
Maybe Jesus can
unlock my lonely heart."

When I became a librarian, I never dreamed I'd search through clothes and personal belongings to retrieve books. At the correctional institution, it was my duty once a month to search the dorm rooms for library books that were apt to be lost or stolen.

While the students were in classes, my aide and I headed for the dorms, which were scattered across a grassy field south of the main building. As we entered a dorm, the guard flicked a switch at the central desk to open all the rooms simultaneously. We rolled our book cart down halls that fanned out like the spokes on a bicycle wheel.

Each tiny room had built-in shelves for storage and a narrow cot with a hard vinyl-covered mattress and a hump at one end for a pillow. There were no sheets, only a scratchy wool blanket and a few personal belongings. We found books scattered everywhere and soon had a loaded book cart.

Since this was a minimum security institution, the rooms were better than the typical prison cell, but they were still sparse. The biggest shock was to see that the boys were allowed to cover their walls, floor to ceiling, with pornographic posters and magazine pictures. A poster of a sports hero or movie star was a rare sight. Only the rooms of the "spacetakers," a term for those being punished for breaking prison rules, had bare walls.

Staff members disagreed on this controversial practice of allowing pornographic displays. Those who argued for it claimed that there was no proof that pornography causes criminal behavior. I was among those who argued that pornography did not help achieve the state's goal of rehabilitation, noting that several of the inmates were convicted rapists and that all of them were minors.

After a book search, a few young men always came to the library and proudly asked, "Did you see my room? I know you were out there."

Much to my surprise, I never got any complaints. I was baffled that they were pleased because I found their rooms extremely depressing. Perhaps they were so lonely that it made them happy to think someone had come to "visit." I realized how much they needed attention and wanted someone to care.

WALLS

"For I know the plans I have for you," declares the LORD, "plans to prosper you and not to harm you, plans to give you hope and a future."

Jeremiah 29:11

Inside these
prison walls,
you're a young man
with a future.
Asking for forgiveness,
you left your crimes
at the front gate.

Other students
lay bricks
of self-pity and boredom.
You read and study,
building
the foundation
for your career.

Every day you climb
over the wall
with your plans
and dreams,
convincing your teachers
there's such a thing
as rehabilitation.

Even though he was locked up in a correctional institution, Lee had dreams. He wanted to be an attorney. He was encouraged that his criminal record as a juvenile would be erased, allowing him to start with a clean slate when he became an adult.

He was intelligent, likable, and articulate. He often did legal research in the library for his case and offered legal advice to others. He was a skilled jailhouse lawyer, respected by his peers for his knowledge of criminal law. I helped him find answers to his reference questions and recommended books to satisfy his thirst for knowledge.

On cold winter days, he would come to the library to talk with me about books he was reading. Sometimes he would teach me jailhouse games, including the ones that he'd made up to keep his quick mind from being bored. All of them could be played alone or with another person.

My favorite was the button game, which required a person to cut off buttons with prongs from a coat. When you rolled the buttons on the table, you earned two points for the buttons that landed with the prong up and one point for those that landed with the prong sideways. If a button rolled on the floor, you had to subtract a point. After several turns, the person with the most points was the winner.

"Just like life—it's all in the way you roll the dice," he'd say, laughing.

When I left the job at the institution, Lee came to tell me good-bye and to thank me for helping him tolerate the walls that enclosed him.

I never saw Lee again or found out what happened to him. But he had the ability to make his dreams come true, with or without the buttons on his coat.

A student who appreciated my help

_____
_____
_____
_____
_____
_____
_____
_____
_____

Times when I encouraged a student's creativity

_____
_____
_____
_____
_____
_____
_____
_____
_____

A situation where I quit controlling and let God take over

_____
_____
_____
_____
_____
_____
_____
_____
_____

Students I learned to accept and understand

_____
_____
_____
_____
_____
_____
_____
_____
_____

Ways I learned to deal effectively with the bureaucracy

_____
_____
_____
_____
_____
_____
_____
_____
_____

How I handled a school policy that I opposed

_____
_____
_____
_____
_____
_____
_____
_____
_____

PART 2

PRIVATE SCHOOL FOR JUVENILE OFFENDERS

Be strong and courageous. Do not be afraid or terrified because of them, for the LORD your God goes with you; he will never leave you nor forsake you.

Deuteronomy 31:6

My most difficult teaching assignment was in a private school for juvenile offenders, located in a rough neighborhood in the inner city. Every morning on my way to work, I would pray for protection, because students came to school with drugs, stolen goods, and weapons. Teachers worked in teams to protect each other from violence and to help control students.

I worked as a reading specialist with high school age students, most of whom could not read beyond second grade level. Students were taught basic reading, math, and language arts to help them catch up. I had only one student whose scores were high enough at the end of the year to qualify him for entrance into a regular high school.

After this job experience, I felt the traditional educational system was inappropriate for at-risk students who are committing crimes. These students need a simpler curriculum starting in elementary school that concentrates on reading, language arts, math, and survival skills, and that allows them to succeed. Most school systems pass them on to higher grades, require them to use textbooks that they can't even read, and constantly let them fail. This is usually the result of state laws that require students to cover specific skills and courses at each grade level. I believe this is one of the major causes of their entry into the criminal justice system, where they learn a different kind of success.

ORDINARY DAY

Finally, be strong in the Lord and in his mighty power. Put on the full armor of God so that you can take your stand against the devil's schemes.

Ephesians 6:10–11

An ordinary day
begins,
sun shining,
birds singing,
classes in session.

Suddenly
a drunk wanders
into the library,
a student pulls a knife
in the rest room,
police bust
a pusher
selling drugs
near the front sidewalk.

Students
and teachers
walk by,
eyes cast down so
they barely notice.

Apprehensively I drove down the brick street lined with debris and broken glass to the school, which was located in one wing of an abandoned high school. It was a decadent inner city neighborhood where criminal activity was rampant.

Teachers parked their cars inside a fenced area. Even with precautions, hubcaps, windshield wipers, and other car accessories were often missing at the end of the day. When I walked up to the door to enter, there were groups of students standing around and smoking.

Every day one boy blocked my way and blew smoke in my face. At first he made me uncomfortable but after I got to know him, I realized that he wanted attention. I'd smile and ask him how he was. Then he'd let me pass. He still jumped in my path every day for the entire year, because it was his way of saying "Good morning."

Compared to the typical public school, no day was ordinary at this school. Teachers had to be extremely flexible because we never knew if what we had planned would be carried out. The disruptions to the learning process were so great that we learned to be grateful for a ten- or fifteen-minute lesson.

One day a boy brought a gun to school, intending to shoot the math teacher. Fortunately someone snitched on him, and the teacher got the gun away without any injuries. Another day a drunk man came into my classroom, pulled up a chair by my desk, and started talking.

One of the biggest problems was the drug pushers who hung out on the corner. Sometimes they would walk up to the classroom windows and motion to our students, who pulled up the windows and jumped out. They were so much stronger than the other teacher and I that we couldn't stop them. The first time this happened, I was flabbergasted.

For serious incidents, we called the police. For minor problems, we asked the social workers who had an office down the hall to intervene.

In this environment, I learned to take one day at a time and lower my expectations, letting students do simple lessons to achieve success.

FORECAST

The entire law is summed up in a single command: "Love
your neighbor as yourself."

Galatians 5:14

Lord,
I didn't forecast
my career
in these
circumstances,

Teaching kids
nobody wants
in the corner
of an old
inner city school.

You never
sent a warning
they'd have addictions
or refuse
to listen.

I can clear
the air
with quick advice
and textbook
solutions.

But you
want me
to sit down
and be willing
to feel their pain,

And do
unto others
as I would
have them
do unto me.

I'm beginning
to understand:
We're all
equal
in your sight.

The first day of classes at the private school, I was shocked at the students' behavior. In the correctional institution, everyone was controlled in a structured system. Here it was the teacher's responsibility to manage a whole classroom of disruptive students.

After the bell rang, the students walked into the room, eyeing me suspiciously. When I asked them to sit down, they mocked me and either sat on top of the desks or stood. Only a few had paper and pencils. When I passed out supplies to the others, some tore the paper and snapped the pencils in half.

Finally I asked one boy to pass out the books. When I told the students the page number, most sat chewing gum, talking, and ignoring me. Others were imitating me and finding my effort to teach very amusing. One girl, high on drugs, put her head down on her desk and went to sleep. Three boys walked over to the windows and crawled out.

Twenty minutes of desperate efforts to get the class to listen resulted only in my tears—tears of frustration, anger, and confusion. How had I ever ended up in a school like *this?* The students thought my tears were funny. Feeling frantic to get away from them, I walked out, asking the other teacher on my team to watch my class.

I rushed to the principal's office, my face red from crying. "You're scared of them and they know it," the principal said. "I know they're difficult, but you have to earn their respect."

After lunch I returned to the classroom. Students were sleepy from the joints they had smoked outside during lunch break. A few listened and worked, while the rest recognized my presence by mocking or pretending I was invisible.

I made it through that day, and each day got a little better. But I was still exasperated by the students' behavior and attitudes. I wanted to quit, but I needed the job. The way I finally earned respect from them was the biggest surprise of my career.

COOL IT

Let us acknowledge the LORD; let us press on to acknowledge him. As surely as the sun rises, he will appear; he will come to us like the winter rains, like the spring rains that water the earth.

Hosea 6:3

Help me
cool it, Lord.
I'm sinking into
these kids' problems,
drowning in my low salary,
flooded with worry
about a student's future.

Weary
of the daily
tasks,
I wade through
paper,
red tape,
negative thoughts.

Help me
care for myself,
pray for guidance,
feel the refreshing mist
of living water,
your grace
and love.

I was still having trouble with discipline after a few weeks on the job. One day while eating lunch in my classroom, I heard a knock. I opened the door and there he stood, a student about six feet tall with liquor on his breath. Hostility oozed out of every pore in his body.

He spit out a racial slur and took the size thirteen tennis shoes he was holding and slapped me in the face with the dirty soles. He was ready to hit me again when I drew back my fist. I was angry!

Wham! I knocked him in the jaw, determined not to let him knock me over or hurt me again. His mouth flew open in surprise as he rubbed his sore jaw and stared at me in disbelief. I was more shocked than he was! If this had been a public school, I would probably have been in trouble, even though I was defending myself.

He walked away as I went to tell the principal. Two boys who were standing in the hall ran outside to tell the other students. The principal was glad to have a reason to expel him. The boy was an alcoholic, often brought a whiskey bottle to school in his jacket pocket, and had instigated numerous fights.

This incident was the turning point in the students' attitudes toward me. I had gained their respect with a language they understood—the language of physical violence. After that day, I vowed that I'd never get angry enough to hit another student and that I'd learn better ways to handle them. I knew that if I treated my students with gentleness and kindness, even those who didn't like me, the Lord would bless me with peace.

OUTCASTS

Do to others as you would have them do to you.

Luke 6:31

We try hard to
avoid
slow learners,
poor kids,
the ones
with addictions.

Better to teach
students
who travel,
have parents
who care,
and books at home.

Who wants
students with
no school supplies,
dirty clothes, and a
street corner
for a home?

Stick them
in a remedial course,
let them sleep
in class,
or hope they transfer
to another school.

Robert came to school late every day and had no intention of learning. He slipped through the door and pranced across the room to model his latest possession, usually a new jacket.

"I bet you ripped off another store," someone said. "Another day, another jacket, huh?"

The class laughed knowingly. I found out quickly that Robert had a reputation as a shoplifter and made money selling what he'd stolen. About once a week he sat down and attempted to work on the assignment. He was fifteen years old and couldn't read a third grade book. His achievement in stealing was far more impressive.

Whenever I phoned Robert's home, his mother never answered or returned my calls. "My mom says she doesn't want to talk to my teachers," he told me.

It was nearly impossible to get Robert to participate in classroom activities. He had experienced so much failure that I felt perhaps I should help him avoid the pain of learning. Trying to read when he was so far behind only discouraged him more. He needed one-to-one tutoring, but there was none available.

Robert was a student I wanted to reach but felt I never did. Unfortunately he seemed headed for a life behind bars.

Like Robert, all the students at this school had criminal records and had not coped well in the public schools. This school was their last chance at getting an education. No matter how rude, unappealing, or shabbily dressed they were, I tried to follow the golden rule and treat them with respect when they were in my classroom. This was a real test of my faith and tenacity.

BOXING MATCH

The Lord is my fort where I can enter and be safe; no one can follow me in and slay me. He is a rugged mountain where I hide; he is my Savior, a rock where none can reach me, and a tower of safety. He is my shield. He is like the strong horn of a mighty fighting bull.

Psalm 18:2 TLB

Two boys
in a knot of anger,
twisted
into hostile words.
Untangling them
will not be easy.

A classroom
forms
the boxing ring.
The social worker
referees.

Fighters prance
and pounce,
eager to win
the heavyweight
title.

Excited students
bounce like
rubber balls
in their
ringside seats.

Pow!
A winner
is announced.
The boys shake
hands and call
it quits.

Today anger
came untied,
when muscles
won out
over wits.

Public school systems usually suspend students who fight, but in the private school the solution was more imaginative and effective. When two boys started a fight, the social worker raced to his office and grabbed two pairs of boxing gloves.

"Push back the desks," he yelled, and everyone pitched in and arranged desks and chairs around the edge of the classroom to form a boxing ring. Then he handed the gloves to the two angry boys who were glaring at each other.

"Fight it out!" he hollered.

The two boys started boxing while the students cheered and clapped, rooting for their favorite. It was great entertainment and helped the boys vent their anger.

When it was obvious that one boy was winning, the social worker declared the winner and made the two boys shake hands.

We then moved the desks back and resumed the lesson. The positive impact of turning potential violence into acceptable behavior by making it a sport was remarkable.

I believe one reason there are so many fights and attacks on teachers today is because there's not enough opportunity for students to vent their energy and feelings in positive ways. Most schools no longer have recess, which gives students a chance for spontaneous movement and action. Organized sports teams, art and drama, and extracurricular activities are often absent or sparse in inner city schools, where they are needed most.

SHATTERED

Be not afraid of sudden fear, neither of the desolation of the wicked, when it cometh. For the LORD shall be thy confidence, and shall keep thy foot from being taken.

Proverbs 3:25–26 KJV

He backed me
against the classroom wall,
a jagged piece of
window glass
pointed at my face
like a dagger.

"What's wrong, Teach?
Scared?" he asked,
a cruel smile curled
across his lips.

I folded myself
into the wall,
praying
for protection.

He paused,
and I could feel
the angry part of him
fighting battles
with his calmer
side.

I heard the glass
shatter,
spilling like
his broken life
in a million
pieces.

Jamaar was an emotionally disturbed boy who lived in a group home. He had been in numerous foster homes after being taken away from his parents, who had abused him severely.

Sometimes he was quiet. He liked maps and would often sit and study the globe after he got his work done. Other times he'd unexpectedly pick up a desk and throw it at the wall. He was so unpredictable that you never knew what might ignite his anger.

Jamaar didn't mix well with the other students, and one day he got up and started bothering them. When I told him to sit down, he became angry. He ran over to the row of windows at the side of the room, one of which had been broken over the weekend by vandals.

He grabbed a piece of window glass, held it like a sword, and started toward me. He got a strange smile on his face as I backed against the wall. The other students were begging him to drop the glass, but he ignored them. I started praying that he'd stop, because I was afraid that he'd stab me in the face. The glass was about two inches from my cheek when he suddenly dropped it.

Two boys had run to get the social worker. The social worker rushed into the room, grabbed Jamaar, and took him out.

This was one of the most frightening incidents of my career, a time when divine intervention saved me. It made me realize that I had to be prepared spiritually for the unexpected, especially in this volatile environment.

CLASSROOM WEAPONS

A man of knowledge uses words with restraint, and a man of understanding is even-tempered.

Proverbs 17:27

A pin inside a spitball,
staples shaped
like wings, or a
paper clip
unfolded like a dart
make perfect
classroom weapons.

Who cares if you
cut a cheek
or hit an eye?

Throw when
the teacher's busy.
Roll your eyes
and look
real innocent.

When you can't
read,
you have to do
something
to pass the time.

The self-fulfilling prophecy has a powerful impact on students. Small words and phrases spoken daily and repeated by teachers are absorbed and stay with students the rest of their lives. I try to think and talk positively to my students, knowing students with low self-esteem or a negative environment are starved for positive feedback.

Juan was a street kid who tried to be like a gangster. He acted tough; wore baggy, stylish clothes; and belonged to a gang. He wore a gold chain with a small gold revolver around his neck.

Underneath his "cool dude" act, I saw a kind, soft-hearted person. He was really lonely and starved for love and attention, but he didn't want his peers to know it.

One day he came to class wearing a tight leather glove on his left hand, the kind of glove robbers use to conceal their fingerprints.

"Take it off and put it away," I said.

"But I don't write with this hand. You just think I'm going to kill somebody," he said defiantly.

"I wasn't thinking anything of the kind. I know you're a loving person with a gentle heart. You would *never* kill anyone!" I said.

He was dumbfounded. Then a look of pride spread over his face. He took off the glove and put it away. The rest of the period, he did his work and hummed a little tune. Once in a while, he would look up from his paper and give me a big smile.

BABE IN ARMS

Like newborn babies, crave pure spiritual milk, so that by
it you may grow up in your salvation, now that you have
tasted that the Lord is good.

1 Peter 2:2–3

She bonded
to me,
a babe in arms.

I spoon-fed
adjectives and adverbs,
doses of poetry,
and stories arranged
like diapers folded
neatly in a box.

At each new discovery
she babbled
and cooed,
as she became
an honor
student.

Months later
she returned,
an unwed
mother,
handing me
her babe in arms.

What
formula
did I fail
to use
when she was
my babe in arms?

Tonya had been adopted by her foster mother, who had a houseful of foster children. "At least somebody wanted me," she said. "But I think she just adopted me to take care of all those little kids. My mom always takes in kids that nobody wants."

Every day after school Tonya diapered AIDS and crack babies and watched the other small children so her mom could have a break.

"My mom pays me," she said, "but sometimes it's too much work. I just need to be a kid."

Tonya was bright and talented and deserved a chance to further her education. I encouraged her, expecting her to be a big success. She was very frustrated about her home situation, but she learned fast and had improved so much that I hoped she'd continue.

My disappointment was intense when she dropped out of school. Later she came back to show me her baby. Tonya was only sixteen, but there wouldn't be time for her to be a kid anymore. She was on welfare, with her own baby to take care of, yet she still lived with her mom and helped with the foster children.

"When my little girl gets older, I'll go back to school," she said apologetically. "I might even go to college."

Now that Tonya had a child to love who needed her, I hoped she'd find a way to make a better life for both of them by finishing her education.

STORMY WEATHER

If any of you lacks wisdom, he should ask God, who gives
generously to all without finding fault, and it will be given
to him. But when he asks, he must believe and not doubt,
because he who doubts is like a wave of the sea, blown
and tossed by the wind.

James 1:5–6

They shift moods
by day, hour, or minute.
I can't predict
the times when they
are uncontrollable
and stormy
or lulled into an
uneasy calm.

The psychologist
warned me
to prepare
for a hurricane.
On good days
I am thankful
for partly cloudy
with a chance of showers.

Just when I see
fair skies
and sun, they roll
into a
thunderbolt,
and lash their violent
moods
into the room.

I wanted Darryl to be absent, but he never was. He was the first one in the classroom every day. In public schools he had been in classes for the emotionally handicapped. Now he was acquiring a criminal record, so he'd enrolled in our school.

His behavior was bizarre. Not a day went by that he didn't do all kinds of things to get attention. Broken paper clips, expertly targeted to hit eyes and faces, would fly across the room from his desk.

"I didn't do it," he'd say, throwing his hands up in the air as if I was pointing a gun at him when I frowned.

He could never get up to turn in an assignment without hitting other students. "I was just swinging my arms, and they got in the way," he'd say.

When caught cheating on a test, he'd deny it and kick the chair. "You don't know how to grade papers right," he'd say. He was so bullheaded that he did the opposite of what I told him. If I said to sit down, he stood up. If I asked him to hurry to his desk and get to work, he'd take baby steps, slowly sit down, and stare at the ceiling.

I couldn't figure out what made him tick, so I started watching him in the halls and the cafeteria. Darryl didn't have one friend. No one wanted to sit by him or talk with him. He was lonely, left out, and selfish. He was an only child and used to getting his own way.

Even if I couldn't help him solve his problems, I needed to find ways to keep him from controlling the whole classroom. First, I ignored his weird remarks and behavior when he wasn't hurting anyone. If he was quiet, did his work, and didn't cheat, I'd give him a reward, usually a Student of the Day certificate.

After discovering that Darryl had mechanical ability, I put him in charge of the audiovisual equipment. If anything needed to be repaired, he'd check it out and tell me what was wrong. When we did group activities, I would ask him to help.

Gradually Darryl improved as he started feeling more important. Sometimes he was still impossible, but I stressed the positive instead of dwelling on his negative behavior.

When dealing with students like Darryl, I have learned to stay calm and do quiet, subtle things to help them feel important and achieve success. I have this belief that all of them are worth saving and that my understanding and concern for them might change their lives and affect their futures.

GRADUATION

No discipline seems pleasant at the time, but painful. Later on, however, it produces a harvest of righteousness and peace for those who have been trained by it.

Hebrews 12:11

Students in
new clothes
march on stage,
mute in unfamiliar
church
surroundings.

Certificates
trimmed in gold
signify
small steps
to improvement.

Attending school
regularly, controlling
one's temper,
being drug-free

are cause for
celebration.

Who said
graduation
meant
getting
a diploma?

Tony entered my class during the second semester. The first day he called me nasty names and put his feet on top of his desk. When I asked him to take them down, he said, "I'll sue you if I have leg problems, because I have a pain in my legs."

When we started the lesson, he tapped his fingers like drumsticks, threw paper wads, and drew gang symbols like the five-point crown on the desktop. What a relief it was when he went to the detention center for two weeks.

After he returned to class, I prayed for a new approach. I had to release my anxiety, or his anger would stir up my own. Then I wouldn't be free to help the other students.

First, I let him run errands for me and take notices to the office. Originally I did it just to get him out of the room. He liked it. It made him feel important so I kept giving him this privilege if he brought school supplies and had a positive attitude.

One day I noticed that he was drawing doodles on his paper; they showed artistic talent. I asked him to make a poster for me, and he did an outstanding job. Soon he had earned a reputation as the "artist-in-residence." The rest of the year I let him make posters and illustrate his assignments. This totally changed his attitude and self-esteem.

At the graduation ceremonies, everyone got a certificate for something. When Tony walked on stage, he was honored with the award for the most improved. On that first day, I never would've dreamed this could happen.

Times when I prayed for protection at work

_____
_____
_____
_____
_____
_____
_____
_____
_____

An experience that surprised me

_____
_____
_____
_____
_____
_____
_____
_____
_____

A student who made great improvement

_____
_____
_____
_____
_____
_____
_____
_____
_____

A school event or situation that was entertaining

_____
_____
_____
_____
_____
_____
_____
_____

A situation where the Lord protected me from harm

_____
_____
_____
_____
_____
_____
_____
_____

Positive qualities I saw in a disruptive student

_____
_____
_____
_____
_____
_____
_____
_____

PART 3

INNER CITY
ELEMENTARY SCHOOL

See, I am sending an angel ahead of you to guard you along the way and to bring you to the place I have prepared.

Exodus 23:20

When I started at this elementary school as a media specialist, the library was filled with worn-out books and materials and the building was in disrepair. It was a depressing environment for faculty and children.

With the arrival of a new principal, restoration of the building, and parental involvement, the school improved 100 percent. School pride, frequent rewards for the students, and money for equipment and books made a tremendous impact. During the four years I worked here, I saw how quickly an inner city school can change. An outstanding school can emerge in any location with any type of students.

I left this school after being robbed at gunpoint in the media center during the school day by two men who had stalked the school looking for a teacher alone. While they held me captive, the door opened. A teacher and her second grade class were standing there, looking like angels in the sunlight. They caused the men to flee with my wallet and keys.

Since this traumatic experience, I have become more aware of school safety. I believe that most schools, especially inner city schools, should have better security because no school is safe anymore. I now pray silently every day after the pledge to the flag that the Lord will protect the students and staff at my school.

STORY HOUR

For the Kingdom of God belongs to men who have hearts
as trusting as these little children's.

Luke 18:16 TLB

I feel like
    a mother hen
with her flock
    as story hour begins.

The children come
    to roost
on the carpeted floor,
    legs folded,
hands in laps, eyes on me.

I scatter seeds
    of beauty, truth,
and love,
    with words and art from
a picture book.

The captive chicks
    grasp each word,
like magic grain,
    and hunger for more.

A class of wiggly first graders could never sit still during story time. Someone was always pulling hair, talking, or playing with Velcro shoe fasteners.

One day as I was reading a picture book in verse about trains traveling across the country, the children caught the rhythm and rhyme of the story. The book *Train Song* by Diane Siebert has catchy words as different kinds of trains go down the track and past cities. Spontaneously the children got up and formed a line, marching across the rug, moving arms back and forth, going "choo-choo" in a whispered tone while I continued reading. At the end of each stanza, one boy hollered, "All aboard!"

While they were moving, the children were smiling and looking at me. It felt as if we were on a real train going on a journey.

As we shared the excitement of words and sounds, I was so tickled that I almost fell off my chair. At the end of the story, the children hugged me and plopped down on the floor, overwhelmed by the joy we had experienced. I never felt frustrated with this class again, because they "taught" me how to enjoy them.

SPACE SHUTTLE SKIES

And pray in the Spirit on all occasions with all kinds of prayers and requests.

Ephesians 6:18

Teachers and children
cluster on the school
patio,
anticipating
a lesson in space.

Eyes peer
heavenward,
spotting
a white streak
across the sky.

Suddenly
a huge cloud
appears,
signaling
an explosion.

Teachers,
stunned by
the tragedy,
herd children
back to classrooms.

Tears flow.
Heads bow.
Today no one argues
against prayer
in the schools.

We often took classes outside to watch the space shuttle soar into space on daytime flights. On January 28, 1986, our students were thrilled that a lesson in space would be taught by a real teacher on the Challenger. Most of them had never known an astronaut, but all of them knew teachers who were special people in their lives.

As we gathered on the school patio on this clear, crisp January day, excited children jumped like popcorn bursting inside a microwave bag and pointed to the white streak in the sky. But something seemed wrong. Suddenly the streak had turned into a big cloud.

"It exploded!" one boy yelled.

"It couldn't!" a girl said. "There was a teacher on board."

Unsure of what had happened, our minds were filled with anxious thoughts. I herded the class I was teaching into the media center and turned on the television set. The announcer confirmed the dreadful news of the accident.

How could such a thing happen? It seemed unreal, but it was true. I couldn't pray out loud with the class, so I asked for a few minutes of silence. Tears were falling on young cheeks as I prayed silently, knowing many children were praying too.

Arguments against school prayer wouldn't have made sense that day. Although the sadness of the tragedy overwhelmed us, it gave me hope that praying in school will never be completely abandoned, even if it is silent.

BOOK BEAR

Train a child in the way he should go, and when he is old he will not turn from it.

Proverbs 22:6

I stir up
a love
for reading
with my
book bear.

He's my recipe
for feeding
children too shy
for a hug,
afraid to trust.

This bundle of fur
and stuffing
snuggles under
soft chins
and melts in tiny arms.

My book bear
proves
that reading and love
are part
of the same brew.

When I use a stuffed animal, an object, or drama to encourage reading, I never know what will happen. Sometimes I get surprising results that bring laughter and joy.

One day Mark and Josh, two boys in the fifth grade class, role-played *How to Eat Fried Worms* by Thomas Rockwell. We had planned this in advance, so Mark had brought in a can filled with earthworms squirming in dirt. He held a worm out to Josh and said, "I dare you to eat this."

Josh had a bottle of ketchup. He poured a few drops on the worm and held it up to his mouth. It was a big fat worm, covered with dirt. At this point everyone expected Josh to toss the worm back in the can or in the wastebasket. Instead, he popped it into his mouth and swallowed it! "Yummy!" he said, patting his stomach.

The boys and girls in the class squealed, giggled, and jumped up and down. They couldn't believe he did it; neither could I!

"Oh, yuck! He ate it!" they yelled.

Mark, holding the can of worms, wanted a good laugh too, so he decided to change the plot. He pulled a huge earthworm covered with dirt out of the can, tossed it into his mouth, and swallowed it! By this time the class was screaming and laughing so loudly that I had to shut the door to keep from disturbing other classes.

After the class had calmed down, Mark grinned, held out the can to me, and said, "Would you like a worm?"

ON TRACK

A student is not above his teacher, but everyone who is fully trained will be like his teacher.

Luke 6:40

A degree
is my ticket
to a paycheck.

I conduct
on crowded trains
with unclear
destinations,
clacking along
with all sorts of baggage.

Passengers fidget
in tidy rows,
stare out the window,
shuffle to another car,
or daydream
in the caboose.

I clean, sweep,
and sort.
I am buried
in mailbags at every
stop.

> Help me
> guide the passengers
> to the right station.

The paper tiger gets more ferocious every week, lining my mailbox, stuffing my files, and packing my desk drawers. Educational companies seem to sprout up overnight, sending catalogs and brochures to peddle their products. New policies and procedures have to be put in writing for legal reasons, and school programs and schedule changes are frequently announced on paper.

Companies selling copy machines and computers promised relief, but these time-saving devices seem to generate more paper. Even with hard drives on my computers, I have to organize the disks, backup disks, and software manuals.

Many times I feel overwhelmed by forms to fill out and bulletins to read. I want to throw them in the wastebasket and shout, "Give me time to teach!" My dilemma over what to discard and what to keep can even become a problem.

I have learned to pray daily for focus and energy so I'll remember that my main purpose is to relate to the students, not be a paper robot. "Time-outs" during the school day have helped me keep my sanity. I stop the lesson early so the children can talk to me or listen to me read a story or poem aloud. On the day we get a class set of newspapers, I give the students time to share and discuss the news. Sometimes I play soft music while they read silently.

When my mail arrives, I toss irrelevant papers and junk mail in the recycling box immediately. I place other papers in color-coded folders and keep a file folder of "current" papers on my desk.

I haven't completely tamed the paper tiger, but I've learned to cope with it more efficiently. This has helped me to be more effective and give the students the attention they deserve.

DREAMS

So we fix our eyes not on what is seen, but on what is unseen. For what is seen is temporary, but what is unseen is eternal.

2 Corinthians 4:18

Dreams float
around
this classroom.

I want to pull them
out of the air,
open them
like a book,
and share them
with the class.

We'll all give
a cheer, shouting,
"Go for it!"
"Don't give up!"
"You can if you
think you can!"

I know dreams
are born
in ordinary schools.

No one knows
how far
a dream may fly.

Father, mold me
into the kind
of teacher
who helps
students
capture dreams.

One way a teacher opens up dreams and possibilities to students is by helping them develop their talents and skills. Whenever a student says, "I want to be an artist when I grow up," or a similar remark, I encourage the dream even if it seems impossible. I want them to realize that hard work, a positive attitude, and caring for others can help them accomplish their goals.

If students show a special talent, I try to find a chance for them to express it at school. I let the ones with drawing talent make posters, enter drawing contests, and make bulletin boards. If a student is a leader, I provide the opportunity for him or her to lead a group activity. I've also held a hobby day in the media center where students display hobbies and collections.

One of my most successful projects emphasized how unique each child is and how much they need each other to develop their skills, fulfill their dreams, and have a happy life. I had all the children in the school, grades K–6, trace their handprint on green construction paper, cut it out, and write their name, age, and birthday on the hand. We taped the hands together in a long chain and hung it on the walls of the school hallway.

The response to our friendship chain from teachers, parents, and visitors was heartwarming, but the response of the children was the most exciting. They enjoyed hunting for their handprint because it made each one feel special. The chain of hands was a touching reminder that they must be a friend and reach out to others to make their dreams come true.

GiFTED CHiLD

Those who are wise will shine like the brightness of the heavens, and those who lead many to righteousness, like the stars for ever and ever.

Daniel 12:3

Inside this crowded classroom,
your sparkling eyes
are shooting stars
across milky ways
of intelligence.

Ideas orbit,
words and numbers spin
the vast space of your mind,
sparking
awesome creations.

I guide
your navigations
into
uncharted
constellations.

Corey greeted me with a smile every morning. He was extremely talented and had a natural ability to get along with all types of kids. He was a wonderful Christian boy with parents who encouraged his activities and his creativity.

Every day after school, he ran about a mile or two in training for marathons and had already won several trophies. He also collected stamps and butterflies and was active in Boy Scouts.

Corey was so clever that I never knew what he would come up with next. He had started a business making unique Native American jewelry pieces using feathers, beads, and arrowheads. Not wanting to waste a minute, he carried a box of supplies in his book bag so he could work on his creations after his class work was done.

When we read legends and folklore of the Native Americans, Corey made a model of a tepee using deerskin and brought it for display. Other students brought in projects too, but his tepee was the most outstanding. Even though Corey knew his was the best, he never compared it to the others aloud. Instead, he complimented the other students on their projects.

All the other kids respected and admired Corey, but he never boasted or called attention to himself. Like a shining star, he was one of those students that I'll never forget.

ANGELS IN THE LIBRARY

Suddenly an angel of the Lord appeared and a light shone in the cell. He struck Peter on the side and woke him up. "Quick, get up!" he said, and the chains fell off Peter's wrists.

Acts 12:7

Lord, thank you
for answering
the intercom today
in an *extraordinary* way.

I used your prayer line
when two robbers
walked in the library,
pointed a gun at me,
and searched my purse
for money and car keys.

You gave me the courage
to stay calm
and sent second grade
angels in the door,
prompting the robbers
to escape.

No one's safe
in school anymore,
but knowing
you have a twenty-four-hour
toll-free number
is all I need.

One morning I was alone in the media center checking in books at a table when two strange men walked in the door. It was a warm day, yet they were bundled up in jackets, stocking caps, and gloves.

"Where's the PE teacher?" the short one asked.

"You'll have to check in at the main office, and they'll tell you," I said, feeling uneasy.

Suddenly the tall one darted across the room, grabbed my left arm, and pointed a silver handgun at my heart.

"Don't move," he said. I was so shocked that my heart pounded and my skin felt clammy. *What are they doing in a school?* I wondered.

"Where's your money?" the other man demanded. I nodded toward the office. He was angry when he discovered that I only had two dollars in my wallet and was wearing silver jewelry instead of gold. As he fumbled through my purse for the car keys, he yelled, "Lie down!"

At first I ignored him, but the second time he yelled I got on my knees and started praying. The other man gripped my arm again and pointed the gun at my head. I had lost all track of time as I prayed for Jesus to save my life.

Suddenly the door flung open and there stood a second grade teacher and her class, ready to come in and check out books. They looked like angels aglow with halos in the bright sunlight.

"Please don't let them shoot the children," I prayed. The two men grabbed my wallet, put away the gun, and walked past the second graders as if nothing had happened. The class had come about three minutes early. Who knows what might have happened if they'd come at the scheduled time?

One of the men was later arrested and convicted in a jury trial. The other one and a third man waiting in a getway truck were never found.

Since that day I have been more awed by the power of prayer to answer our needs in ways only the Lord understands. Before the robbery, I took my life and the lives of others for granted. Now every morning when I awake, I look at each new day as a gift.

I look at the sky more, noticing the clouds, the colors in a sunset, and a rainbow arching across the sky. I cherish the little things: a smile, an act of kindness, and the voices of my loved ones. I can't buy these in a store or order them from a catalog. They are gifts, simple and free, and they're given to each of us every day.

A school-wide activity that I enjoyed

_____

_____

_____

_____

_____

_____

_____

_____

_____

A book or story that I shared with my students

_____

_____

_____

_____

_____

_____

_____

_____

_____

Parents who did something thoughtful

_____

_____

_____

_____

_____

_____

_____

_____

_____

A moment when I experienced God taking over

_____
_____
_____
_____
_____
_____
_____
_____
_____
_____

Concerns I had about school safety

_____
_____
_____
_____
_____
_____
_____
_____
_____

Times when prayer helped me or my students

_____
_____
_____
_____
_____
_____
_____
_____
_____

PART *4*

INNER CITY
JUNIOR HIGH SCHOOL

Consider it pure joy, my brothers, whenever you face trials of many kinds, because you know that the testing of your faith develops perseverance.

James 1:2–3

I worked as a reading specialist at a junior high school in a large school district. The inner city school was across from housing projects in a high-crime area. Students came on the bus from the suburbs or walked from the surrounding neighborhood.

When I came to this school, the building was run-down and the equipment and library were inadequate. After the school was renovated and new materials and furniture were purchased, the school spirit and morale improved among staff and students.

Many of my students read below grade level and had low self-esteem. The majority of those who were committing crimes were frequently absent or suspended, because they wouldn't behave when they were at school. The drop-out prevention programs, while effective, could only handle a few because of lack of funding and personnel.

We need a federal program, similar to Headstart, targeted for students in inner city schools who are committing crimes. In the program, these students would be able to develop marketable skills and earn credit with an easier curriculum and grading system. How much better and more cost effective it would be to help young people become a success, even if it meant lowering the qualifications, than to see them spend the rest of their lives behind bars.

STITCHED IN HOPE

"'If you can'?" said Jesus. "Everything is possible for him who believes."

Mark 9:23

This neighborhood
    is
a crazy quilt
    in haphazard
squares.

Skyscrapers,
huge bobbins of crystal
    and stone,
cast mocking shadows
on housing projects,
    dropped
like patches
on crowded land.

Mothers on welfare
    rock babies
on front steps
    to the rhythm
of boom boxes.

Police cars
   baste
      zig
  zag
      seams through bullets
and needles.

Students
   stretch elastic minds
around ideas
and numbers,
   stitched in hope
like the flag
   waving at the
front door.

I have one rule in my classroom: "Show respect." It covers every problem that comes up. At the beginning of the school year, I ask my students to look up the definition for respect. *Webster's* says respect means to feel or show reverence for others. We then discuss what it means to show respect for ourselves, our classmates and teachers, and our learning materials and school.

Students watch teachers' actions, attitudes, and expressions, so I have a watchful audience checking on my "respect." If I want them to behave respectfully, I must set the example.

In the fall I always have several students who talk when we say the pledge to the flag. I cannot legally require them to say the pledge, but I expect them to be quiet. I pass out a copy of the Bill of Rights and we talk about the freedoms for which the flag stands. After this lesson, they are much more willing to show respect for our flag.

Whenever a student calls another a derogatory name, I remind them of our respect rule. I remind myself that I shouldn't call them silent names either.

By the middle of the year I see great progress; this does wonders for my hopefulness. Knowing that name-calling is out and perfection isn't possible but worth striving toward, most students try hard to please me and impress me with their respectful attitude.

LAYAWAY PLAN

We have different gifts, according to the grace given us. If a man's gift is prophesying, let him use it in proportion to his faith. If it is serving, let him serve; if it is teaching, let him teach.

Romans 12:6–7

I'm a teacher
on layaway,
until the period
is over,
and I get a break,

until the week
passes,
and I can
enjoy
the weekend,

until the year
ends,
and I can
transfer to
another school.

I said I'd not
live in the future,
but my career
comes
in monthly installments.

I mark
the days,
awaiting vacation,
as interest accumulates
on the account.

Teaching is so exhausting that some days I feel like I'm making payments on goods that never get delivered. But most of the time I'm so familiar with the stress that I accept it as normal. Others who are unaccustomed to controlling a group of students have a different perspective. Their feedback makes me realize how much strength and courage it takes to be an effective teacher.

A substitute teacher left this note on my desk following my half-day absence:

Ms. Nichols,
   Well, for only two hours of class, that sure was a long day! For both classes, my attempts to keep the "students" from sharing answers and/or just plain cheating on the prefix quiz were futile. I'm sure that more cheated than were caught. At least fourth period finished the first three assignments, in spite of all of the noise. Fifth period could not even keep quiet or stop throwing things (erasers, staples, etc.) long enough to read the story, so I sent for the assistant principal. She had a sturdy voice and gave them the work that is on the board (written in red), and she asked me to bring it to her at

the end of the day. When she left the room, she took two of the troublemakers (Pierre and Ryan) with her.

You asked me to leave my social security number so that you could request me for any future absences. I am not leaving it because I don't think I'm right for your class. (For example, I have no formal training as a truancy officer or in mob control.) Thanks for the thought.

Joe Smitz

P.S. Ryan did not return a black pen he borrowed.

THE PEARL

Again, the kingdom of heaven is like a merchant looking
for fine pearls. When he found one of great value, he went
away and sold everything he had and bought it.

Matthew 13:45–46

My students' minds
are tight
like
clams.

Some stay shut,
a few lift
a crack,
then close me out.

Suddenly
one opens wide,
revealing
a precious gem.

Help me,
Father,
reach
the pearl.

When Frederick transferred from another school, he refused to work, sat and scowled at me, or put his head down and went to sleep.

"Go ahead and waste your time in school. Who needs an education anyway?" I'd say.

Gradually he began to participate by "accidentally" getting involved in our discussions, plays, and computer work. I'd praise him in quiet ways because I knew he had to "save face" and pretend to be a rebel.

By the third nine-week period, I was pleased with his progress in attitude, effort, and grades. He was completely different than when he arrived, but I still saw room for improving his conduct.

I called him to my desk to give him a scholarship warning, which is a written notice to the parents that if a student does not improve either academic grades or conduct, he or she may not pass for the nine weeks. Frederick got down on his knees beside my chair and begged, "Please don't give me one. I'm already grounded. I'll do better, you know I will. You're my friend!"

I always give my students a second chance, sometimes more. I tore the scholarship warning in little shreds and threw it in the wastebasket. Frederick folded his hands, bowed his head, and said softly, "Thank you, Lord."

I never had problems with him again.

METAMORPHOSIS

Therefore, if anyone is in Christ, he is a new creation; the
old has gone, the new has come.

2 Corinthians 5:17

Wrapped
in my cocoon,
I sip coffee, and
squirm through
morning rush hour.

School buses,
like giant
caterpillars,
line the parking
lot.

I pull up,
gather tote
and lunch bag,
slinking through
crowded halls.

Each period my
students swoop
into the classroom
on youthful
wings.

We create
a living nest,
reaching advanced
stages of
metamorphosis.

At day's end,
I return
to my cocoon and
face the crawl
toward home.

I used to dread the morning rush hour and felt exhausted by the time I got to school. Honking horns, gas fumes, and semi-trucks caused too much stress. I started praying for an answer to my bad mood.

One day on my way to work I noticed beautiful sunbeams coming through fluffy clouds and colorful snapdragons growing beside a motel parking lot. I remembered walking my grandma, who was blind, to the garden when I was a child. She always asked me to pick a bouquet for her.

I would hold the flowers up to her nose and describe them as she sniffed them and touched them lovingly with her wrinkled hands. "They're beautiful," she'd say. "And it's such a nice sunny day, isn't it?"

My bad mood began to change, and I said, "Thank you, Lord, that I can see the sky and the pretty flowers growing near the interstate. Forgive me for being so ungrateful."

What a difference changing my attitude made. I started leaving earlier for work and didn't feel so rushed. Every day I tried to count at least one blessing. I remembered my grandma and how difficult her life was because she couldn't see. No matter how challenging the circumstances, counting my blessings and putting my faith in Jesus always leads to sunshine. When I get too wrapped up in my own answers, I become blind to the good things around me.

MORNING DUTY

Arise, shine, for your light has come, and the glory of the
LORD rises upon you.

Isaiah 60:1

Seagulls ease me
   into the morning.

Flying in a dot-to-dot pattern
   above the school roof,
their rhythmic caws are
   my wake-up call.

They swoop
   into my morning duty,
unaware of their
   role.

Students wait
   for the bell
in their own numbered
   sequence.

I am a crayon
trying to connect.

Usually my morning duty starts peacefully as I watch students climb off the buses that bring them to the inner city. Occasionally the day starts in an uproar.

One morning I had been on duty for fifteen minutes and had already stopped one fight and broken up another. As the bell rang, I entered the building, holding two students on either side of me so that they wouldn't continue to hit each other. Suddenly I saw about a hundred students who had lingered after the bell running across the patio and grass to the sidewalk.

When I reached the crowd, I saw two boys lying on the sidewalk pounding each other. The dean arrived, pulled them apart, and took them to the office. I followed with the two boys I had caught earlier. They were suspended for ten days, a normal procedure.

I know one teacher who has a permanent jaw injury, another with a back injury, and a third with a neck injury from breaking up student fights on school grounds. All of these incidents occurred at other schools, and I constantly hear other true stories of teachers injured by students.

Violence and disrespect toward teachers is not just in inner city schools. It is happening everywhere, in both elementary and secondary schools across the country.

Every year more students seem to come to class without supplies, use foul language, and talk back to teachers. Numerous times I have seen a child misbehave at school, yet the parent takes the child's part. We will not be able to improve the academics in our nation's schools until we make discipline a national priority and set legal guidelines that students and parents must follow.

BE MY BUDDY

Suppose a man comes into your meeting wearing a gold ring and fine clothes, and a poor man in shabby clothes also comes in. If you show special attention to the man wearing fine clothes and say, "Here's a good seat for you," but say to the poor man, "You stand there" or "Sit on the floor by my feet," have you not discriminated among yourselves and become judges with evil thoughts?

James 2:2–3

Michelle walks to
    the end of the line,
torn book bag on her shoulder,
    smudge spots on her dress,
thick glasses
    taped at the temple.

She grabs a breakfast tray,
    walks to a table
lined with girls dressed
    in spandex tights,
neon earrings, and
    carbon copy smiles.

"Go away. Don't
   sit here," they chirp.
Michelle gulps
   her orange juice,
stuffs a biscuit in her pocket,
   and heads for my duty post.

"Be my buddy," she says.
   "You're my favorite teacher."
The girls walk by
   on their way to class,
noses turned up
   like trumpets in a marching band.

Michelle looks down
   at her dirty shoes.
I know
   all she wants
is a buddy
   her own age.

Just as Jesus heals us, we teachers must be healers in
the classroom. This can be a painful process and requires
patience, not instant solutions.

Sometimes the attitudes of students need healing. The
young people in my class often pick on a certain student
because of a disability, a speech defect, or another qual-
ity that is different. I let them know immediately that I will
not tolerate any name-calling or prejudice.

Tim was a sweet boy with thick glasses, a learning disability, and a stutter. The other students made fun of him
and snickered every time he answered a question.

The first time he was absent, I talked to them about their attitude and behavior toward him.

"We all have problems that we are trying to overcome, because none of us is perfect," I said. "When you have a problem that everybody notices, do you like people to laugh when you try to improve?"

After our talk, they changed their attitude toward Tim and the snickering subsided. One day Tim answered a question fluently.

One boy, who had often ridiculed him, said, "Tim, you talk real good when you slow down."

"That's because Tim knows we are his friends, and none of us will make fun of him," I said.

The whole class sat there watching Tim smile from ear to ear.

It was a tender moment, one I'll always remember.

PROJECT TIME

Whatever you do, work at it with all your heart, as working for the Lord, not for men, since you know that you will
receive an inheritance from the Lord as a reward. It is the
Lord Christ you are serving.

Colossians 3:23–24

Father,
I'm awed
by the power
to decide what
young people learn.

My students
read books,
take notes,
and create
a project.

On the due date,
they turn in
the finished products,
watching
for my reaction.

My smile
and enthusiasm
are as important
as the
grades.

Grant me
the courage
to use this power
wisely, knowing
they'll remember
the rest of their lives.

Ronnie hated school, teachers, and himself. The first day of summer school, he said, "When I grow up, I'm going to be a teacher like you so I can sit around and do nothing all day."

He insulted the other students, did very little work, and was a constant disruption.

When I called his mother, I found out that his grandpa and aunt were both dying of cancer, and that his dad had lost his job. Because Ronnie had so much stress at home, I decided to pray specifically for him every day. I visualized Jesus giving him a hug, patting him on the shoulder, and cheering for him. I gave him frequent rewards and compliments, let him use the computer to do his work, and encouraged him to use his sense of humor in a positive way.

He was a good artist so I had him write his own dictionary and illustrate each word. He liked the project so much that he even started working on it at home. Although it didn't happen overnight, I saw a remarkable improvement in Ronnie's work habits and behavior. His mother told me that she couldn't believe how much he had improved his attitude toward school.

By the end of summer school, he had the highest average in the class. On the last day of school, he wrote a note in my keepsake book. It said: "Don't forget me. I was the one who *tried* to drive you crazy."

GENERATION GAP

Train a child in the way he should go, and when he is old he will not turn from it.

Proverbs 22:6

We are alike,
yet different,
teachers and students,
parents and children.

Look at the forest
of pine trees,
giant toothpicks
nudging the soil,
feathering the sky.

Their offspring
sit in a jar
on the table,
tiny slivers
picking our teeth.

Who would
guess
we are made of
the same wood?

One day a comment in class triggered a discussion about the juvenile prison where I'd worked. As I started telling my students dramatic stories of my experiences, they were so interested that we spent the whole period talking and never got to the lesson.

I explained the daily routine in a prison, the twenty-four-hour monitoring, and aspects of the prison culture that make it dramatically different from a life of freedom. The prison brought up issues closely related to these kids' lives.

Orlando, who is already accumulating a criminal record, was extremely attentive. Usually he goofs around, seldom works, and tries to start fights. He's always been unreachable, but this particular day he opened up. He ran up to my desk and told me the names of all the gangs in the city, how each gang signifies with their hands, and how he steals CDs and cars.

"Do your parents know you're in a gang?" I asked him.

"It's a secret," he said. "But my dad was in one when he was young."

He proudly showed me a 14-karat gold revolver charm on a chain around his neck and another one on his key chain.

"Why guns?" I asked.

"I love them!" he said. "You have to have a real one to survive."

I asked him about laws to control gun sales. He told me that they won't make any difference.

"We get them on the black market," he said.

This boy is only thirteen years old, and I've known many others like him. He is street smart yet lacking in basic skills. He can't read a fourth grade book or write a complete sentence. He's in seventh grade for the second time and still doesn't know his math facts. No wonder he gets straight Fs on his report card.

Several times I've called his dad, who acts like he's concerned about Orlando's school performance. Yet Orlando never improves as a result of my phone calls.

After that day, Orlando talked to me even though he knew I didn't approve of his activities. I felt sorry for him, because he didn't know any other way of life or how to feel important without his gang and his crimes. I'm not sure I helped him, but it seemed to make him feel better to have an adult listen.

Be happy, young man, while you are young, and let your
heart give you joy in the days of your youth.

Ecclesiastes 11:9

There's a party
in the halls
between periods.

Invitations were sent out,
everybody came to chat,
bang lockers,
pick fights, and
hold hands.

Students bounce
up
   and
       d
         o
           w
             n
the stairs,
like balloons,
celebrating five minutes
of freedom.

Teachers on hall duty
recall days
as smooth-skinned youth,

when they had
enough energy
to throw
a party
every hour.

Charlie is a real character who smiles continually, makes funny noises, chases the girls, and entertains while at school. He wears big bloomer pants fashioned with crazy prints, black-and-white zigzags, and other such beguiling noticeables. He seldom has a pencil or paper, and he loves to talk.

Because he is so affable, it is nearly impossible for Charlie to arouse my anger. We have a chair in the reading lab that is on casters. That chair is just Charlie's speed. He rolls all over the lab in the chair when he thinks I'm not watching.

He is particularly fond of rolling up to the table where Lisa and Jessica are working. He has developed a repertoire of noises that he uses to get their attention.

Yesterday Jessica said, "Just leave us alone so we can get our work done."

"But I just want to embrace your book!" he said, grabbing a book and hugging it.

Recently after I helped him with an assignment, he rolled over to the fan, placed his hands on the stem, and pretended it was a microphone. "Thank you! Thank you for your support!" he said in a deep voice.

I have also seen him in the hall bumping kids he doesn't even know on the shoulder. When they turn to object, he grins and waves at them.

Charlie wants everyone's worries and troubles to go away. He wants life to be joyful and fun, so he does all he can to make it that way.

MIGRATION

Who are these that fly along like clouds, like doves to their
nests?

Isaiah 60:8

The first week
students flock
into the school
on silent feathers,
soft voices fluttering
through the hallways.

They declare
territories,
harbor friends,
make enemies,
and settle
for a long winter.

In springtime
they chirp and
caw, fly from
limb to limb,
or embrace as
lovebirds.

The last day
tears of familiarity
reflect loss
and growth
as they sprout wings
and fly away.

At the beginning of each school year, my students are like young birds needing love, understanding, and care. After months of learning and growing together, we form a close bond.

To commemorate our relationship, I ask each student to contribute to a keepsake book at the end of the school year. They trace their handprint on paper and decorate it to reflect their personality. After listing vital statistics (name, age, height, weight, eye color, hair color), they add special qualities they want me to remember. Some draw a watch, a ring, or another distinguishing mark.

Under the handprint I ask them to write something they liked about my class. I am always amazed at what they say because it is seldom what I expected. The students who gave me the most trouble make the most touching comments. They almost always mention little things I said or did that made them feel special.

One boy with learning disabilities wrote, "I like your Student of the Day awards because my grandma gives me 50 cents for them and hangs them on the wall." A girl whose dad rejected her after a divorce said, "You understood when I was upset about my dad and let me put my head down or go in the workroom and cry."

Another student, a hyperactive boy who had low self-esteem, noted, "I liked it that you let me use the computer a lot. Now I'm a computer whiz." And one girl wrote poetry about her dad dying of cancer. On the last day she wrote me a poem expressing her feelings about leaving my class.

> Goodbye, goodbye
>   my tears go down,
> goodbye, goodbye
>   you're a great teacher,
> goodbye, goodbye,
>   my heart is dying.
> Goodbye.

There is one statement I hear every year, one that means the most to me because so many of my students have said it. It is simply, "Thank you for being my friend."

When I look back at my keepsake books, I am reminded of how much power a teacher has to change lives. That's why I need Jesus by my side every day.

A student who spread joy and laughter

_____
_____
_____
_____
_____
_____
_____
_____
_____

A class that improved greatly in attitude and behavior

_____
_____
_____
_____
_____
_____
_____
_____
_____

Times when I prayed for strength to keep going

_____
_____
_____
_____
_____
_____
_____
_____
_____

A student's behavior or speech that shocked me

_____

_____

_____

_____

_____

_____

_____

_____

_____

A time when I closed the generation gap

_____

_____

_____

_____

_____

_____

_____

_____

_____

End of the year activities that were memorable

_____

_____

_____

_____

_____

_____

_____

_____

_____

Judy Nichols, a certified reading teacher, media specialist, and classroom teacher, writes out of her experiences in working in inner city schools and in other difficult settings—a private school for juvenile offenders and a state correctional institution. She is currently a reading specialist at Stewart Middle School, an inner city school in Tampa. Her publication credits include features in *The Wisconsin State Journal & The Capital-Times* (Madison, Wisconsin), articles in *Learning, Gifted Children's Newsletter, Tampa Bay Magazine,* and *Instructor,* and poems in *Hopscotch Magazine for Girls* and other magazines.